Holiday Sweets

by Michelle Prater Burke

Contents

Cover photograph: Gingerbread Cookies (page 26) made by using gingerbread men and women cookie cutters and decorating appropriately.

IDEALS PUBLICATIONS INCORPORATED
NASHVILLE, TENNESSEE

New Year's Eve

Easy Banana Tiramisu
Makes 12 servings

1½ cups milk
2 tablespoons instant coffee granules
1 8-ounce package cream cheese, softened
¼ cup sugar
1 package (4-serving size) instant vanilla pudding and pie filling
2 cups frozen whipped topping, thawed
3 ripe bananas, sliced
1 6-ounce package ladyfingers, split and cut in half
1½ ounces semisweet chocolate, grated
Banana slices for garnish
Chocolate shavings for garnish

In a small bowl, stir together milk and coffee until coffee is almost dissolved; set aside. In a large bowl, beat together cream cheese and sugar until smooth and blended. Stir in pudding mix; gradually beat in coffee mixture until smooth and blended. Fold in whipped topping and 3 sliced bananas until just blended; set aside.

Layer a third of the ladyfingers on bottom and sides of a 3-quart serving dish. Evenly spoon in a third of the cream cheese mixture and sprinkle with half of the grated chocolate. Repeat layers, ending with cream cheese mixture. Chill at least 1 hour before serving. Garnish with additional banana slices and chocolate shavings.

Winter Cranberry Tart
Makes 15 to 18 servings

Crust:
2½ cups flour
⅓ cup firmly packed brown sugar
½ teaspoon salt
10 tablespoons melted butter

Filling:
⅔ cup firmly packed brown sugar
¼ cup melted butter
3 eggs, beaten
⅔ cup light corn syrup
1 tablespoon cornstarch
½ teaspoon salt
1 teaspoon vanilla
1¼ cups coarsely chopped cranberries
1 cup coarsely chopped walnuts

Preheat oven to 350° F. To make crust, in a large bowl, combine flour, brown sugar, and salt. Using a fork, cut in butter until mixture resembles coarse crumbs. Press firmly onto bottom and 1 inch up sides of a greased 13-by-9-by-2-inch baking pan. Bake 20 minutes.

To make filling, in a large bowl, combine brown sugar, butter, eggs, corn syrup, cornstarch, salt, and vanilla; stir until smooth. Stir in cranberries and walnuts. Pour mixture over baked crust. Bake 25 minutes or until filling is set. Cool on wire rack. Store covered in refrigerator.

Reduced-Fat Chocolate Orange Cake
Makes 15 servings

2 cups flour
1 teaspoon baking soda
½ teaspoon salt
⅔ cup lower-fat margarine
1 cup packed, light brown sugar
4 egg whites
1 cup skim milk
1 tablespoon orange juice
2 cups quick-cooking rolled oats
1 tablespoon freshly grated orange peel
1 12-ounce package reduced-fat, semisweet chocolate chips

Preheat oven to 350° F. Spray a 13-by-9-by-2-inch baking pan with vegetable cooking spray; set aside. In a small bowl, sift together flour, baking soda, and salt; set aside. In a large bowl, cream margarine with brown sugar. Add egg whites, skim milk, and orange juice; mix well. Add flour mixture and mix well. Stir in oats, orange peel, and chocolate chips. Spread in prepared pan. Bake 25 to 30 or until light golden brown and center feels firm when touched lightly. Cool completely on wire rack.

Reduced-Fat Chocolate Frosting

1 cup reduced-fat, semisweet chocolate chips
1 cup powdered sugar
3 tablespoons skim milk

In a small microwave-safe bowl, place chocolate chips. Microwave at high power (100%) 45 seconds; stir until melted. Gradually add powdered sugar and milk, beating with wire whisk. If necessary, microwave an additional 30 to 45 seconds or until mixture is smooth when beaten. Spread immediately.

Crispy Crunchy Brittle
Makes 1½ pounds

2 cups coarsely chopped walnuts
1 cup sugar
½ cup corn syrup
¼ cup water
1 tablespoon butter
½ teaspoon salt
1 teaspoon baking soda

Grease a 15-by-10-inch jelly roll pan; set aside. In a 9-inch, glass pie pan, spread walnuts. Microwave at high power (100%) 2½ minutes; stir. Microwave an additional 2½ minutes; set aside. In a 2-quart glass measuring bowl with handle, combine sugar, corn syrup, water, butter, and salt. Microwave at high power (100%), stirring occasionally, 5 to 6 minutes or until sugar is dissolved. Stirring every 2 minutes, microwave an additional 4½ to 7 minutes or until mixture reaches 300° F on a candy thermometer. Add baking soda, mix well. Stir in walnuts. Immediately pour mixture into prepared jelly roll pan, spreading evenly. Cool; break into pieces.

Rice Pudding
Makes 4 servings

1½ cups cooked rice
⅓ cup sugar
¼ teaspoon salt
2 cups milk, divided
1 egg, beaten
⅔ cup raisins
1 tablespoon butter
½ teaspoon vanilla
   Dash nutmeg or cinnamon

In a heavy saucepan, combine rice, sugar, salt, and 1½ cups of the milk. Place over medium heat, stirring occasionally, 15 to 20 minutes or until thick and creamy. In a small bowl, blend egg and remaining ½ cup milk; stir into rice mixture. Stir in raisins. Cook an additional 2 minutes, stirring constantly. Stir in butter and vanilla. Spoon into serving dishes. Sprinkle with nutmeg or cinnamon.

FLOURISHES: *Lacy white icing designs look wonderful atop chocolate desserts. Using a pastry bag filled with icing and fitted with a writing tip, draw small designs or flowers onto wax paper. Allow to dry overnight, then carefully peel the lacy designs from the wax paper and arrange on dessert.*

Hot Caramel Spoon 'n' Bake
Makes 6 to 8 servings

    1   cup flour
    1½ teaspoons baking powder
    ¼   teaspoon salt
    ⅔   cup sugar
    1   cup raisins
    ½   cup milk
    2   cups water
    1   cup firmly packed brown sugar
    2   tablespoons butter
        Whipped cream

Preheat oven to 350° F. In a small bowl, sift together flour, baking powder, and salt; set aside. In a large bowl, combine sugar, raisins, and milk. Add flour mixture and stir just until moistened. Spread batter into a greased, 9-inch-square baking pan and set aside. In a medium saucepan, combine water, brown sugar, and butter. Place over medium heat, stirring frequently, until sugar is dissolved and butter is melted. Carefully pour hot mixture over batter (the syrup will be thin). Bake 30 to 40 minutes. Serve warm, spooning out cake and turning upside down. Top with whipped cream.

Chewy Butterscotch Walnut Bars
Makes 16 bars

    1¼ cups graham cracker crumbs
    1   cup sugar, divided
    ½   cup melted butter, divided
    2   eggs
    1   package (4-serving size) instant butterscotch
        pudding and pie filling
    1   cup flour
    ½   cup chopped walnuts
    ½   cup semisweet chocolate chips

Preheat oven to 375° F. In a small bowl, combine crumbs, ¼ cup of the sugar, and ⅓ cup of the melted butter; mix well. Press mixture onto bottom of a 9-by-9-by-2-inch baking pan. Bake 8 minutes; set aside.

Reduce oven temperature to 350° F. In a medium bowl, with electric mixer on high speed, beat eggs and remaining ¾ cup sugar until mixture is thick and pale yellow. Add remaining butter. Stir in pudding mix and flour until blended. Stir in walnuts and chocolate chips. Spread mixture over baked crust. Bake 30 minutes. Cool; cut into bars.

Reduced-Fat Chocolate Brownies
Makes 3 dozen

    ¾   cup cocoa
    ½   teaspoon baking soda
    ⅔   cup melted lower-fat margarine, divided
    ½   cup boiling water
    2   cups sugar
    3   egg whites, slightly beaten
    1   teaspoon vanilla
    1⅓ cups flour
    ¼   teaspoon salt
    1   cup reduced-fat, semisweet chocolate chips

Preheat oven to 350° F. Spray a 13-by-9-inch baking pan with vegetable cooking spray; set aside. In a large bowl, sift together cocoa and baking soda; stir in ⅓ cup of the melted margarine. Add boiling water; stir until mixture thickens. Stir in sugar, egg whites, vanilla, and remaining ⅓ cup melted margarine; stir until smooth. Add flour and salt; blend completely. Stir in chocolate chips; pour into prepared pan. Bake 30 to 35 minutes or until brownies begin to pull away from sides of pan. Cool completely in pan on wire rack. Cut into squares.

Valentine's Day

Chocolate-Banana-Strawberry Torte
Makes 8 servings

- ½ cup flour
- 4 teaspoons cocoa
- 1 teaspoon baking powder
- 3 eggs, separated
- 1 cup sugar
- 1 ripe banana, mashed (about ⅓ cup)
- ⅛ teaspoon salt
- 2 firm bananas, sliced
- 1 cup sliced strawberries
-   Powdered sugar

Preheat oven to 325° F. Spray a 10-inch springform pan with vegetable cooking spray; set aside. In a small bowl, sift together flour, cocoa, and baking powder; set aside. In a large bowl, beat egg yolks and sugar until mixture is pale and thick. Stir in flour mixture and mashed banana; set aside.

In a medium bowl, beat egg whites until foamy. Add salt; beat until stiff peaks form (do not overbeat). Fold half of the egg whites into banana mixture until blended; fold in remaining egg whites. Pour batter into prepared pan. Bake 35 to 40 minutes or until wooden pick inserted in center comes out clean. Run knife around edge of pan; release. Cool completely on wire rack.

Just before serving, arrange sliced bananas and strawberries on top of torte. Dust with powdered sugar.

Norwegian Molasses Cookies
Makes 4 dozen

- 2¼ cups flour
- 2 teaspoons baking soda
- ¾ cup butter, softened
- 1 cup firmly packed, light brown sugar
- ¼ cup egg substitute
- ¼ cup light or dark molasses
- ¼ cup sugar
- 1 cup powdered sugar
- 5½ teaspoons skim milk
-   Colored sprinkles

Preheat oven to 350° F. In a small bowl, sift together flour and baking soda; set aside. In a large bowl, with electric mixer on medium speed, cream butter with brown sugar until light and fluffy. Add egg substitute and molasses, beating until smooth. Stir in flour mixture. Cover; chill 1 hour.

Shape dough into forty-eight 1¼-inch balls; roll balls in sugar. Place 2 inches apart on greased and floured baking sheets. Lightly sprinkle balls with water. Bake 15 to 18 minutes. Cool on wire racks. In a small bowl, combine powdered sugar and milk. Spread mixture on cookies and decorate with colored sprinkles.

FLOURISHES: *Make desserts memorable by topping them with a dusting of powdered sugar. For a change from the traditional paper doily, place a holiday craft stencil atop your dessert before sifting with powdered sugar. To add color to a white dessert, add a small amount of cocoa to the sugar before sifting.*

Chocolate Lovers' Cherry Cake and
Cherry Vanilla Chip Brownies (page 8)

Chocolate Lovers' Cherry Cake
Makes 10 to 12 servings

¾ cup coarsely chopped slivered almonds, divided
1 18¼-ounce package yellow cake with pudding mix
¼ cup cocoa
¼ cup sugar
2 eggs
¼ cup vegetable oil
2 teaspoons almond extract
1 21-ounce can cherry pie filling
1 cup semisweet chocolate chips

Preheat oven to 350° F. Grease and flour a 10-inch bundt pan. Sprinkle ¼ cup of the almonds evenly in bottom of pan; set aside. In a large bowl, stir together cake mix, cocoa, and sugar. Add eggs, oil, almond extract, and cherry pie filling; beat until well blended and cherries are chopped. Stir in remaining ½ cup almonds and the chocolate chips; pour into pan. Bake 55 to 60 minutes or until wooden pick inserted in center comes out clean. Cool in pan 10 minutes; invert cake onto wire rack and cool completely.

Cherry Vanilla Chip Brownies
Makes 16 brownies

½ cup chopped maraschino cherries, well drained
⅔ cup flour
⅓ cup cocoa
¼ teaspoon baking powder
⅓ cup butter, softened
¾ cup sugar
2 eggs
2 tablespoons light corn syrup
1 teaspoon vanilla
1 teaspoon almond extract
⅓ cup chopped, slivered almonds
1 cup vanilla chips
Vanilla Chip Drizzle (recipe follows)
Maraschino cherry halves, well drained

Preheat oven to 350° F. Line an 8-inch-square baking pan with foil; grease and flour foil and set aside. Lightly press chopped cherries between layers of paper towels to remove excess moisture; set aside.

In a small bowl, sift together flour, cocoa, and baking powder; set aside. In a large bowl, cream butter with sugar until light and fluffy. Add eggs, corn syrup, vanilla, and almond extract; stir well. Add flour mixture and blend until combined. Stir in chopped cherries, almonds, and vanilla chips. Pour batter into prepared pan. Bake 25 to 30 minutes or until brownies begin to pull away from sides of pan. Cool completely in pan. Cover; refrigerate until firm. Remove from pan; cut into shapes with cookie cutters or cut into squares. Garnish with Vanilla Chip Drizzle and cherry halves. Refrigerate until drizzle is firm; refrigerate any remaining portions.

Vanilla Chip Drizzle

⅔ cup vanilla chips
1 teaspoon shortening

In a small microwave-safe bowl, place vanilla milk chips and shortening. Microwave at high power (100%) 30 seconds; stir. If necessary, microwave an additional 15 seconds until chips are melted when stirred. Using tines of fork, drizzle mixture across Cherry Vanilla Chip Brownies.

FLOURISHES: *A graceful chocolate curl adds a perfect, decadent touch to any special dessert. To make curls of your own, use a bar of milk chocolate or white chocolate that is at room temperature. Draw a vegetable peeler across the chocolate at an angle.*

Cherry Vanilla Fudge
Makes about 1½ pounds

- 2 tablespoons butter
- 2 cups sugar
- ½ cup sour cream
- ⅓ cup light corn syrup
- ¼ teaspoon salt
- 2 teaspoons vanilla
- ½ cup quartered candied cherries
- 1 cup coarsely chopped walnuts

Grease an 8½-by-4½-inch loaf pan; set aside. In a 2-quart glass measuring bowl with handle, cream butter with sugar until light and fluffy. Add sour cream, corn syrup, and salt; stir well. Microwave at high power (100%) 5 minutes; stir to dissolve sugar. Microwave 6 minutes or until mixture reaches 236° F on a candy thermometer. Let stand 15 minutes; do not stir. Add vanilla; beat 6 minutes or until mixture starts to lose its gloss. Stir in cherries and walnuts; quickly pour into prepared pan. Cool; cut into squares.

Sweetheart Cookie Puzzle
Makes two 10-inch cookies

- 2 cups quick-cooking rolled oats
- 1¼ cups flour
- 1 cup butter, softened
- ½ cup sugar
- 1 teaspoon vanilla
  Assorted small candies

Preheat oven to 350° F. In a medium bowl, combine oats and flour; set aside. In a large bowl, cream butter with sugar until light and fluffy. Add oat mixture and vanilla and stir well. Divide dough in half. On lightly greased baking sheets, mold each half into a heart shape about ¼-inch thick. To decorate, gently press candy pieces into dough. Using a sharp knife, cut dough into 8 to 10 random shapes to form puzzle pieces (do not separate pieces). Bake 18 to 20 minutes or until lightly browned. Using a knife, carefully separate pieces. Cool 5 minutes on baking sheets; remove to wire racks to cool completely.

Black-Bottom Pie
Makes 8 servings

- 1 cup graham cracker crumbs
- 3 tablespoons sugar
- ⅔ cup melted butter, divided
- 4 1-ounce squares semisweet chocolate
- 1 package (4-serving size) instant vanilla pudding and pie filling
- 1 cup cold milk
- 1 cup sour cream

In a small bowl, combine crumbs, sugar, and ⅓ cup of the butter. Press onto bottom and side of an 8- or 9-inch pie pan; set aside. In a small saucepan, melt chocolate and remaining ⅓ cup butter over medium heat, stirring until smooth. Spread mixture into prepared crust; chill. In a large bowl, prepare pudding according to package directions using 1 cup milk; stir in sour cream. Spread into crust. Chill at least 2 hours.

Almond Chocolate Kiss Cookies
Makes 2 dozen

- 1 cup flour
- 1 teaspoon baking soda
- ½ cup butter, softened
- ½ cup sugar
- 1 egg
- 1 teaspoon almond extract
- ⅓ cup toasted, slivered almonds
- 24 chocolate candy KISSES

Preheat oven to 350° F. In a small bowl, sift together flour and baking soda; set aside. In a large bowl, with electric mixer on medium speed, cream butter with sugar until light and fluffy. Blend in egg and almond extract. Add flour mixture. Wrap dough in plastic wrap; freeze for 15 minutes. Shape dough into 1-inch balls; roll balls in toasted almonds. Place 2 inches apart on ungreased baking sheets. Bake 7 to 9 minutes or until lightly golden. Before cookies cool, top each with a chocolate KISS, pressing lightly into center of each cookie. Cool on wire racks.

Easter Sunday

Spring-into-Easter Cutouts
Makes 4 dozen

2½ cups flour
1 teaspoon baking soda
½ teaspoon salt
1 cup quick-cooking rolled oats
1 cup butter, softened
1 cup sugar
1 egg
2 tablespoons milk
1 teaspoon vanilla
Assorted small candies or colored sugar
Egg Glaze (recipe follows)

In a medium bowl, sift together flour, baking soda, and salt; add oats and set aside. In a large bowl, cream butter with sugar until light and fluffy. Add egg, milk, and vanilla; beat well. Add flour mixture and mix well. Divide dough in half. Cover; chill 2 to 3 hours.

Preheat oven to 350° F. On a lightly floured surface, roll out dough to ⅛-inch thickness. Cut with assorted floured 2- to 3-inch Easter-shaped cookie cutters. Place cookies on an ungreased baking sheet. Decorate with small candies, colored sugar, and Egg Glaze. Bake 8 to 10 minutes or until edges are light golden brown. Cool 1 minute on baking sheet; remove to wire racks to cool completely.

Egg Glaze

1 egg yolk
¼ teaspoon water
Food color

In a small bowl, combine egg yolk and water. Divide mixture into 3 small bowls and tint with food color. Using a small brush, paint glaze on Spring-into-Easter Cutouts before baking.

Citrus Streusel Squares
Makes 2½ dozen

2½ cups flour
2 teaspoons baking powder
1 teaspoon salt
2 cups quick-cooking rolled oats
1 cup butter, softened
1½ cups firmly packed brown sugar
1 14-ounce can sweetened condensed milk
¼ cup lemon juice
¼ cup orange juice
2 teaspoons grated lemon peel
2 teaspoons grated orange peel
Powdered sugar

Preheat oven to 350° F. In a medium bowl, sift together flour, baking powder, and salt. Add oats and set aside. In a large bowl, cream butter with brown sugar until light and fluffy. Add flour mixture; mix until crumbly. Reserve 2 cups of oat mixture for streusel. Press remaining oat mixture onto bottom of an ungreased 13-by-9-inch baking pan.

In a small bowl, combine condensed milk, lemon juice, orange juice, lemon peel, and orange peel; mix well. Spread mixture evenly over crust. Sprinkle with reserved oat mixture, patting gently. Bake 35 to 40 minutes or until light golden brown; cool completely. Sprinkle with powdered sugar. Cut into bars.

Citrus Streusel Squares and
Spring-into-Easter Cutouts

Hot Fudge Topsy Turvy
Makes 6 servings

1 cup flour
2 teaspoons baking powder
¼ teaspoon salt
8 tablespoons cocoa, divided
¾ cup milk
1 teaspoon vanilla
2 tablespoons melted butter
1 cup sugar, divided
1 cup raisins
½ cup firmly packed brown sugar
1½ cups water

Preheat oven to 350° F. In a medium bowl, sift together flour, baking powder, salt, and 2 tablespoons of the cocoa; set aside. In a large bowl, combine milk, vanilla, butter, and ⅔ cup of the sugar. Add flour mixture and stir well. Stir in raisins. Spoon batter into a greased, 8-inch-square baking pan. In a small saucepan, combine remaining 6 tablespoons cocoa, remaining ⅓ cup sugar, brown sugar, and water. Place over high heat, stirring constantly; bring to a full boil. Carefully pour hot mixture over batter in pan. Bake 40 minutes or until wooden pick inserted in center comes out clean. Cool 10 minutes. Serve warm, spooning out cake and turning upside down.

Spring Surprise
Chocolate Cupcakes
Makes 1½ dozen

1¼ cups flour
⅓ cup cocoa
½ teaspoon baking soda
1 cup sugar
¾ cup water
½ cup vegetable oil
1 egg
1 teaspoon vanilla
Surprise Filling (recipe follows)
Flaked coconut

Preheat oven to 350° F. Place 18 paper liners (2½ inches in diameter) in muffin pans. In a medium bowl, sift together flour, cocoa, and baking soda; set aside. In a large bowl, combine sugar, water, oil, egg, and vanilla. Add flour mixture; beat until smooth. Fill muffin cups two-thirds full with batter. Prepare Surprise Filling; spoon about 1 tablespoon filling over batter in each cup. Bake 25 to 30 minutes or until wooden pick inserted in center comes out clean. Cool completely on wire racks. Garnish with coconut.

Surprise Filling

1 8-ounce package cream cheese, softened
⅓ cup sugar
1 egg
½ cup flaked coconut
Food color

In a medium bowl, combine cream cheese, sugar, and egg; beat well. Stir in coconut. Stir in few drops food color.

Cookie Pie
Makes 12 servings

½ cup butter, softened
¾ cup firmly packed brown sugar
2 eggs
1 teaspoon vanilla
½ cup flour
1 6-ounce package semisweet chocolate chips
1 cup large walnut pieces
1 9-inch, unbaked pie shell
Vanilla ice cream

Preheat oven to 325° F. In a large bowl, cream butter with brown sugar until light and fluffy. Add eggs and vanilla; beat well. Stir in flour; mix well. Stir in chocolate chips and walnuts; pour into unbaked pie shell. Bake in lower third of oven 50 to 55 minutes or until top is golden brown. Serve warm with vanilla ice cream.

Country Lemon Tart
Makes 8 to 10 servings

Crust:
- ½ cup butter, softened
- 3 tablespoons powdered sugar
- 1¼ cups flour
- 1 egg yolk
- ⅓ cup finely chopped pecans
- ¼ teaspoon salt

Filling:
- 3 eggs, beaten
- 1 cup sugar
- 1 tablespoon flour
- 3 tablespoons lemon juice
- 1½ teaspoons grated lemon peel
- Powdered sugar

Preheat oven to 350° F. To prepare crust, in a large bowl, cream butter with powdered sugar until light and fluffy. Add flour, egg yolk, pecans, and salt. Blend with a fork. Form dough into a ball. Dust fingertips with flour. Press dough evenly onto bottom and up side of a lightly greased, 9-inch pie pan. Bake 10 minutes.

To prepare filling, in a large bowl, combine eggs, sugar, flour, lemon juice, and lemon peel; stir until smooth. Pour into baked crust. Bake 20 to 25 minutes or until filling is set. Cool completely on wire rack. Dust lightly with powdered sugar.

Lemon Drizzle Cake
Makes 12 servings

- 3 cups flour
- 2 teaspoons baking powder
- ¼ teaspoon salt
- 1 cup butter, softened
- 2¾ cups sugar, divided
- 4 eggs
- 1 cup sour cream
- 1 tablespoon grated lemon peel
- 1½ cups raisins
- ⅓ cup lemon juice

Preheat oven to 350° F. In a medium bowl, sift together flour, baking powder, and salt; set aside. In a large bowl, cream butter with 2 cups of the sugar until light and fluffy. Add eggs; beat well. Stir in flour mixture alternately with sour cream; blend well. Stir in lemon peel and raisins. Pour batter into a greased and floured, 10-inch tube pan. Bake 1 hour and 15 minutes or until wooden pick inserted in center comes out clean. Cool 10 minutes in pan on wire rack. Place on cake plate. In a small bowl, combine lemon juice and remaining ¾ cup sugar; blend well. Brush mixture on hot cake; cool.

Cocoa-Coconut Oatmeal Nests
Makes about 4 dozen

- 2 cups flour
- ¼ cup cocoa
- 1 teaspoon baking soda
- ½ teaspoon salt
- ¾ cup butter, softened
- ¾ cup sugar
- ¾ cup packed, light brown sugar
- 2 eggs
- 1 teaspoon vanilla
- 1½ cups flaked coconut
- 1½ cups quick-cooking rolled oats
- Miniature, candy-coated chocolate eggs

Preheat oven to 350° F. In a medium bowl, sift together flour, cocoa, baking soda, and salt; set aside. In a large bowl, cream butter with sugar and brown sugar until light and fluffy; beat in eggs and vanilla. Add flour mixture; mix well. Stir in coconut and oats. Drop batter by heaping teaspoons onto an ungreased baking sheet. Bake 8 minutes or until set. Cool slightly; remove to wire racks to cool. Press chocolate egg into center of each cookie. Cool completely.

FLOURISHES: *Use a rolling pin to flatten a gumdrop into a circle. Cut the circle in half and roll up each half to create a gumdrop rosette—the perfect garnish for a favorite spring dessert.*

Mother's Day

Light and Luscious Strawberry Cheesecake
Makes 14 servings

1½ cups graham cracker crumbs
3 tablespoons melted butter
1 15-ounce package part-skim ricotta cheese
⅔ cup flour
4 eggs, separated
2 tablespoons grated lemon peel
2 teaspoons vanilla
1 cup sugar, divided
1 cup nonfat sour cream
3 pints strawberries, hulled and divided
4 teaspoons lemon juice
¼ cup red currant jelly, melted

Preheat oven to 300° F. In a medium bowl, combine crumbs and butter. Press mixture onto bottom and 2 inches up the side of a lightly greased, 9-inch springform pan; set aside. In a large bowl, beat ricotta cheese until smooth. Add flour, egg yolks, lemon peel, vanilla, and ¾ cup of the sugar; mix well. Stir in sour cream and blend thoroughly. In a medium bowl, beat egg whites until stiff but not dry; fold into cheese mixture. Pour into prepared crust; smooth top. Bake 1 hour. Turn off oven; cool in oven 1 hour with door ajar. Remove from oven and chill thoroughly.

Purée 2 pints strawberries with the remaining ¼ cup sugar and the lemon juice; strain sauce to remove seeds. Cover and chill. To serve, halve remaining strawberries and arrange on top of cake. Brush strawberries with melted jelly. Cut cake into wedges and serve with sauce.

It's-the-Berries Chocolate Tart
Makes 10 to 12 servings

¾ cup butter, softened
½ cup powdered sugar
1½ cups flour
½ cup milk
2 egg yolks, beaten
¼ cup sugar
¼ teaspoon salt
2 cups chocolate chips
1 pint strawberries, hulled

Preheat oven to 350° F. In a small bowl, cream butter with powdered sugar until light and fluffy; stir in flour. Press mixture onto bottom and side of a 9½-inch, round tart pan with removable bottom. Bake 20 to 25 minutes or until lightly browned; cool completely.

In a medium microwave-safe bowl, microwave milk at high power (100%) 1 to 1½ minutes until hot but not boiling. With wire whisk, stir in egg yolks, sugar, and salt. Microwave 30 seconds at a time, stirring after each heating, until mixture is hot, smooth, and slightly thickened. Stir in chocolate chips until melted and mixture is smooth. Pour into prepared crust. Place plastic wrap directly onto surface of tart; refrigerate until firm.

To serve, remove plastic wrap. Slice strawberries and arrange over top of tart. Serve cold; refrigerate any remaining portions.

Light and Luscious
Strawberry Cheesecake

Chocolate Cherry Cake
Makes 10 to 12 servings

2 10-ounce jars maraschino cherries without stems, drained, rinsed, and divided
1¾ cups flour
¾ cup cocoa
1½ teaspoons baking soda
⅔ cup butter, softened
1¾ cups sugar
2 eggs
1 teaspoon almond extract
1 teaspoon vanilla
1½ cups sour cream
Whipped Cream Filling (recipe follows)

Preheat oven to 350° F. Lightly press cherries between layers of paper towels to remove excess moisture. In a small bowl, sift together flour, cocoa, and baking soda; set aside. In a large bowl, cream butter with sugar until light and fluffy. Add eggs, almond extract, and vanilla; beat well. Stir in flour mixture alternately with sour cream, stirring after each addition. Beat until well blended. Pour into 2 greased and floured, 9-inch, round cake pans. Bake 30 to 35 minutes or until wooden pick inserted in center comes out clean. Cool 10 minutes; remove from pans to wire racks to cool completely.

Prepare Whipped Cream Filling. To assemble, place one cake layer, rounded side down, on serving plate. Spread with ½-inch-high layer of filling. Reserve 12 cherries; place remaining cherries over top, leaving 1 inch around edge free of cherries. Place second cake layer, rounded side up, on top; spread remaining filling on top. Cover; refrigerate until serving time. Garnish with reserved cherries. Cover; refrigerate any remaining portions.

Whipped Cream Filling

2 cups cold whipping cream
⅓ cup powdered sugar
1 teaspoon almond extract

In a large bowl, beat whipping cream, sugar, and almond extract until stiff. Use immediately.

Butter Tart Treasures
Makes 1 dozen

Pastry for 2 pie shells
¾ cup raisins
¼ cup butter, softened
½ cup firmly packed brown sugar
½ cup light corn syrup
1 egg, beaten
1 teaspoon vanilla
¼ teaspoon salt

Preheat oven to 425° F. On floured surface, roll pastry out thin; cut into twelve 4-inch rounds. Place rounds into medium-sized muffin cups (2¾ inches in diameter). Evenly divide raisins among shells. In a medium bowl, cream butter with brown sugar until light and fluffy. Add corn syrup, egg, vanilla, and salt; blend well. Pour mixture into muffin cups, filling two-thirds full. Bake on lowest oven rack 12 to 15 minutes or just until set. Cool on wire rack.

Russian Raisin Teacakes
Makes 4 dozen

1 cup butter, softened
¼ cup powdered sugar
1 teaspoon vanilla
2 cups flour
1 cup walnuts
1 cup raisins, chopped
Additional powdered sugar

Preheat oven to 350° F. In a large bowl, cream butter with ¼ cup powdered sugar and vanilla until light and fluffy. Stir in flour, walnuts, and raisins. Cover; refrigerate until firm. Shape dough into 1-inch balls. Place on ungreased cookie sheets. Bake 10 minutes in upper third of oven. Roll warm cookies in powdered sugar. Cool; roll again in powdered sugar.

Chiffon Cake
Makes 12 servings

2¼ cups flour
1 tablespoon baking powder
¼ teaspoon salt
1½ cups sugar
½ cup vegetable oil
7 eggs, separated
1 teaspoon vanilla
¾ cup cold water
2 teaspoons finely shredded orange peel
1 teaspoon finely shredded lemon peel
½ teaspoon cream of tartar
   Fluffy White Frosting (recipe follows)

Preheat oven to 325° F. In a large bowl, sift together flour, baking powder, and salt. Stir in sugar and make a well in the center of mixture. Add oil, egg yolks, vanilla, and water. With electric mixer on low speed, beat 5 minutes or until satin smooth. Fold in orange and lemon peels; set aside.

Thoroughly wash beaters. In a very large bowl, with mixer on medium to high speed, beat egg whites and cream of tartar until stiff peaks form. Pour egg yolk mixture in a thin stream over egg white mixture and gently fold in. Gently pour batter into an ungreased, 10-inch tube pan. Bake 65 to 70 minutes or until top springs back when lightly touched. Immediately invert cake in pan onto cake plate; cool completely. Using a narrow metal spatula, loosen the sides of the cake from the pan to remove. Frost with Fluffy White Frosting.

Fluffy White Frosting
Makes about 4 cups

1 cup sugar
⅓ cup water
¼ teaspoon cream of tartar
2 egg whites
1 teaspoon vanilla

In a small saucepan, combine sugar, water, and cream of tartar. Place over medium-high heat and bring mixture to a boil, stirring constantly until sugar dissolves.

In a medium bowl, combine egg whites and vanilla. While beating with electric mixture on high speed, very slowly add the sugar mixture. Beat 7 minutes or until stiff peaks form.

Raspberry-Almond Thumbprint Cookies
Makes about 6 dozen

1 cup butter, softened
1 cup powdered sugar
½ teaspoon salt
2 teaspoons almond extract
2 cups flour
½ cup finely chopped almonds
⅓ cup raspberry jam
1 2-ounce white confection baking bar
   (white bark or white chocolate)

Preheat oven to 350° F. In a large bowl, cream butter with powdered sugar until light and fluffy. Add salt and almond extract. Stir in flour and mix well. Shape dough into 1½-inch balls. Roll balls in almonds; place 2 inches apart on ungreased baking sheets. Make a depression in the center of each cookie with your thumb. Bake 12 to 16 minutes or until edges are lightly browned. Make a deeper depression in cookie immediately after removing from oven if necessary. Fill depression with ¼ teaspoon raspberry jam or enough to fill center of cookie.

In a double boiler, melt white confection baking bar. Pour melted confection into a plastic bag. Clip off one end of the plastic bag and drizzle confection over cookies to glaze.

FLOURISHES: Scatter crystallized flowers over cakes and cupcakes for instant elegance. To make, hold an edible blossom (such as a violet or pansy) with tweezers and brush the surface with diluted egg white. Sprinkle with superfine sugar and dry on wax paper for several days.

Independence Day

Red, White, and Blueberry Bars
Makes about 2 dozen

Crust:
- ¾ cup flour
- ¼ teaspoon baking soda
- ¼ teaspoon salt
- ⅓ cup firmly packed brown sugar
- 1 cup quick-cooking rolled oats
- ¼ cup chopped nuts
- ⅓ cup melted butter

Filling and Topping:
- 2 8-ounce packages cream cheese, softened
- ¾ cup sugar
- 2 tablespoons flour
- 2 eggs
- 1 teaspoon vanilla
- 2 cups blueberries
- ½ cup strawberry preserves

Preheat oven to 350° F. To make crust, in a large bowl, sift together flour, baking soda, and salt. Add brown sugar, oats, and nuts; mix well. Add butter; mix until crumbly. Press mixture onto bottom of a lightly greased, 13-by-9-inch baking pan. Bake 10 minutes.

To make filling, in a large bowl, beat together cream cheese, sugar, and flour until smooth. Add eggs and vanilla; beat well. Pour mixture over baked crust and spread evenly. Bake 25 minutes or until set. Cool completely; chill. In a small bowl, combine blueberries and preserves. To serve, cut bars into squares and top with fruit. Refrigerate any remaining portions.

All-American Banana Split
Makes 1 serving

- 1 firm banana, cut in half lengthwise
- 1 scoop each of chocolate, strawberry, and vanilla ice cream
- 2 tablespoons butterscotch topping
- 2 tablespoons chocolate syrup
- 1 tablespoon chopped pecans or walnuts
  Whipped cream
- 1 maraschino cherry

Place banana halves in an individual dessert dish. Arrange ice cream between banana halves. Drizzle butterscotch topping and chocolate syrup over ice cream. Sprinkle with nuts; top with whipped cream and cherry.

Orange Creamsicle Pie
Makes 8 servings

- 1¼ cups graham cracker crumbs
- ¼ cup sugar
- ⅓ cup melted butter
- 1 quart frozen vanilla yogurt, softened
- 1 6-ounce can frozen orange-juice concentrate, thawed
  Whipped topping
  Orange slices

In a small bowl, combine crumbs, sugar, and butter; mix well. Press mixture onto bottom and side of a 9-inch pie pan. Set aside. In a large bowl, with electric mixer on medium speed, blend yogurt and orange juice; spread into prepared crust. Freeze 4 hours or until firm. To serve, garnish with whipped topping and orange slices.

Rocky Road Frozen Sandwiches
Makes 9 sandwiches

 1 package (6-serving size) instant chocolate
     pudding and pie filling
1½ cups milk
 2 cups frozen whipped topping, thawed
 ½ cup semisweet chocolate chips
 ½ cup miniature marshmallows
 ⅓ cup chopped walnuts
18 graham crackers

In a large bowl, prepare pudding according to package directions using 1½ cups milk. Fold in whipped topping, chocolate chips, marshmallows, and walnuts. Arrange 9 graham crackers in a 9-by-9-inch baking pan. Spread pudding mixture evenly over grahams; top with remaining grahams. Freeze 4 to 6 hours or until firm. To serve, cut into squares.

Mock Apple Pie
Makes 8 servings

     Pastry for 9-inch, 2-crust pie
1¾ cups butter-flavor cracker crumbs
 2 cups water
 2 cups sugar
 2 teaspoons cream of tartar
 2 tablespoons lemon juice
     Grated rind of 1 lemon
 2 tablespoons butter
 ½ teaspoon ground cinnamon

Preheat oven to 425° F. Roll out half the pastry and line a 9-inch pie pan. Spread crackers in bottom of prepared crust. In a medium saucepan, combine water, sugar, and cream of tartar. Place over high heat; bring to a boil. Reduce temperature and simmer for 15 minutes. Add lemon juice and rind; cool. Pour syrup over crackers. Dot with butter; sprinkle with cinnamon. Roll out remaining pastry; place over pie. Trim, seal, and flute edges. Slit top crust to allow steam to escape. Bake 30 to 35 minutes or until crust is crisp and golden. Cool completely.

Pineapple Summer Shortcakes
Makes 4 servings

 1 8-ounce can pineapple chunks or slices
 1 3-ounce package cream cheese, softened
 1 tablespoon honey
 ½ teaspoon grated lemon peel
 1 teaspoon lemon juice
 4 individual shortcakes or 4 generous
     slices pound cake
     Assorted sliced fresh fruit, such as strawberries,
     nectarines, raspberries, or blueberries

Drain pineapple; reserve 1 tablespoon juice. In a medium bowl, beat together cream cheese, honey, lemon peel, lemon juice, and reserved juice until blended and smooth. Spoon filling evenly into center of shortcakes or over pound cake slices. Arrange pineapple and fruit over filling.

Razzy Rhubarb Crisp
Makes 8 servings

19 graham crackers, divided
 2 cups chopped rhubarb
 1 10-ounce package frozen raspberries
     in syrup, thawed
 2 tablespoons cornstarch
 ⅔ cup firmly packed, light brown sugar, divided
 ⅓ cup flour
 ¼ cup melted butter

Preheat oven to 375° F. Place 9 graham crackers on bottom of an 8-by-8-by-2-inch baking pan; set aside. In a medium saucepan, combine rhubarb, raspberries, cornstarch, and ½ cup of the sugar. Place over medium heat until mixture thickens and begins to boil. Spoon into prepared pan; set aside. In a large bowl, crush remaining graham crackers into coarse crumbs. Stir in flour, butter, and remaining sugar. Sprinkle mixture over fruit. Bake 20 to 25 minutes or until hot and bubbly. Cool slightly; serve warm.

Great American Brownie Cherry Pie
Makes 8 to 10 servings

⅓ cup chopped maraschino cherries without stems, well drained
⅔ cup flour
⅓ cup cocoa
¼ teaspoon baking powder
½ cup butter, softened
¾ cup sugar
2 eggs
2 tablespoons light corn syrup
2 teaspoons almond extract
⅓ cup coarsely chopped slivered almonds
1 cup vanilla chips
Frozen whipped topping, thawed
Additional maraschino cherries, with stems, well drained

Preheat oven to 325° F. Grease and flour a 9-inch, round, glass pie plate; set aside. Lightly press chopped cherries between layers of paper towels to remove excess moisture; set aside. In a small bowl, sift together flour, cocoa, and baking powder; set aside. In a medium bowl, cream butter with sugar until light and fluffy. Add eggs, corn syrup, and almond extract. Add flour mixture and beat well. Stir in chopped cherries, almonds, and vanilla chips. Pour into prepared pan. Bake 30 to 35 minutes or until set. Cool completely in pan on wire rack. Cover; refrigerate until serving time. Garnish with whipped topping and cherries. Refrigerate any remaining portions.

Chocolate Strawberry Shortcake
Makes 8 servings

6 cups fresh strawberries, divided
¾ cup sugar, divided
1⅔ cups flour
⅓ cup cocoa
1 tablespoon baking powder
¼ teaspoon salt
½ cup butter
⅔ cup milk
1 egg, beaten
1 cup cold whipping cream
2 tablespoons powdered sugar

Preheat oven to 450° F. Reserve 6 whole strawberries. Slice remaining berries. In a large bowl, gently stir together sliced berries and ¼ cup of the sugar; set aside. In a large bowl, sift together flour, cocoa, baking powder, and salt. Stir in remaining ½ cup sugar. Cut in butter until mixture resembles coarse crumbs. In a small bowl, combine milk and egg; beat well with wire whisk. Add milk mixture all at once to flour mixture, stirring just until moistened. Spread dough into a greased, 8-inch, round baking pan, building up edge slightly. Bake 15 to 18 minutes or until wooden pick inserted in center comes out clean; cool 10 minutes. Remove from pan; place on serving plate.

Beat whipping cream and powdered sugar until stiff. Arrange some sliced berries over cake; top with whipping cream mixture. Garnish with reserved whole strawberries and serve with remaining sliced strawberries.

Peach Raisin Cobbler
Makes 6 servings

1 cup flour
1½ teaspoons baking powder
¼ teaspoon salt
1¼ cups sugar, divided
1 cup milk
½ cup melted butter
2 cups peeled, sliced peaches
1 cup raisins
1 teaspoon ground cinnamon
¼ teaspoon ground nutmeg
¼ teaspoon allspice

Preheat oven to 350° F. In a large bowl, sift together flour, baking powder, and salt. Stir in 1 cup of the sugar. Blend in milk and butter. Pour batter into a greased, 9-inch-square pan. In a large bowl, combine peaches, raisins, remaining ¼ cup sugar, cinnamon, nutmeg, and allspice; toss to coat evenly. Spoon peach mixture evenly over batter. Bake 45 minutes or until lightly browned.

Thanksgiving

Choco-Topped Butterscotch 'n' Spice Cake
Makes about 12 servings

1   18¼-ounce package yellow cake mix
1   package (4-serving size) instant vanilla pudding and pie filling
4   eggs
1   cup canned pumpkin
½   cup water
⅓   cup vegetable oil
1   tablespoon ground pumpkin pie spice
1   10-ounce package butterscotch chips
4   1-ounce bars bittersweet baking chocolate
1   teaspoon shortening

Preheat oven to 350° F. Grease and flour a 12-cup bundt pan; set aside. In a large bowl, combine cake mix, pudding mix, eggs, pumpkin, water, oil, and pumpkin pie spice; beat until well combined. Spoon 2 cups batter onto bottom of prepared pan. Into remaining batter, stir butterscotch chips; spoon evenly into prepared pan over previous batter. Bake 50 to 55 minutes or until wooden pick inserted in center comes out clean. Cool in pan on wire rack 20 minutes. Invert cake onto wire rack; cool completely.

Break chocolate into pieces. In a small microwave-safe bowl, place chocolate and shortening. Microwave at high power (100%) 1 minute or until mixture is melted and smooth when stirred. Immediately spoon topping over entire top of cake. Let stand until firm.

Easy Chocolate Coconut Cream Pie
Makes 8 servings

1   9-inch pie shell
1   package (4-serving size) vanilla cook and serve pudding and pie filling mix (do not use instant pudding mix)
½   cup sugar
¼   cup cocoa
1¾ cups milk
1   cup flaked coconut
2   cups frozen whipped topping, thawed

Bake pie shell; set aside to cool completely. In a large microwave-safe bowl, stir together dry pudding mix, sugar, and cocoa. With a wire whisk, stir in milk until blended. Microwave at high power (100%) 6 minutes, stirring every 2 minutes with wire whisk, until mixture boils and is thickened and smooth. If necessary, microwave an additional 1 minute; stir.

Cool 5 minutes in bowl; stir in coconut. Pour into baked pie shell. Carefully press plastic wrap directly onto pie filling. Cool; refrigerate 6 hours or until firm. Top with whipped topping.

FLOURISHES: *Chocolate leaves are an easy yet always impressive garnish. Using a small paint brush, brush several coats of melted chocolate on the underside of fresh, nontoxic leaves (mint, lemon, and ivy leaves work well). Place leaves on wax paper (chocolate side up) and chill until hardened. Gently peel away the leaves before using.*

Choco-Topped Butterscotch 'n' Spice Cake and
Easy Chocolate Coconut Cream Pie

Chocolate Date Tartlets
Makes 2 dozen

Filling:
- ¼ cup sugar
- 1 8-ounce package chopped dates
- 1 tablespoon cocoa
- 1 tablespoon cornstarch
- 3 tablespoons butter
- ½ cup water
- 24 small walnut halves

Crust:
- 1 3-ounce package cream cheese, softened
- ½ cup butter, softened
- 1 cup flour
- ½ cup ground walnuts

To prepare filling, in a small bowl, combine sugar, dates, cocoa, and cornstarch; set aside. In a medium saucepan, melt butter. Remove from heat and stir in date mixture and water. Return to heat. Cook, stirring constantly, 3 to 5 minutes or until thickened. Set aside.

Preheat oven to 375° F. To prepare crust, in a large bowl, blend cream cheese and butter. Add flour and mix well. Stir in walnuts. Divide dough into 24 equal balls. Press onto bottoms and up sides of ungreased miniature muffin cups. Fill each with cooled date mixture. Top each with walnut half. Bake 20 to 25 minutes or until crust is lightly browned. Cool completely in pans on wire rack. Carefully remove tartlets with tip of paring knife.

Cumberland Apple Tart with Oat Crust
Makes 8 to 10 servings

- 2 large golden delicious apples, peeled and thinly sliced (about 3 cups)
- Juice of half a lemon
- ½ cup butter, softened
- ¼ cup brown sugar
- 1 cup flour
- ¼ cup quick-cooking rolled oats
- ½ cup finely chopped pecans
- ½ cup sugar
- ½ teaspoon ground cinnamon

Preheat oven to 375° F. In a large bowl, toss apple slices with lemon juice; set aside. In a large bowl, with electric mixer, cream butter with brown sugar until light and fluffy. Add flour and oats and mix well. Stir in pecans. Form dough into a ball. Dust fingertips with flour and press dough onto bottom and up side of a lightly greased, 9-inch pie pan. Arrange apple slices evenly over crust in circular pattern starting from outside edge and working toward the middle. Fill in any gaps until all apple slices are used. In a small bowl, combine sugar and cinnamon and sprinkle evenly over apples. Bake 35 to 40 minutes or until crust is lightly browned and apples are tender. Cool on wire rack.

Applesauce Spice Bars
Makes 2 dozen

- 2 cups flour
- ½ teaspoon baking soda
- 1 teaspoon ground cinnamon
- 1 teaspoon allspice
- ¼ teaspoon salt
- ½ cup butter, softened
- 1 cup firmly packed brown sugar
- 1 egg
- 1 cup applesauce
- 1 cup chopped walnuts
- 1 cup raisins
- 1½ cups powdered sugar
- 2 tablespoons milk
- ½ teaspoon vanilla

Preheat oven to 350° F. In a small bowl, sift together flour, baking soda, cinnamon, allspice, and salt; set aside. In a large bowl, cream butter with brown sugar until light and fluffy. Add egg; beat well. Add flour mixture alternately with applesauce; mix well. Stir in walnuts and raisins. Spread batter into a greased, 13-by-9-inch baking pan. Bake 20 to 25 minutes or until golden brown. Cool 5 minutes.

In a small bowl, combine powdered sugar, milk, and vanilla; blend well. Spread over warm surface. Cool completely; cut into bars.

Pumpkin Walnut Cookies
Makes about 4 dozen

2½ cups flour
1   tablespoon baking powder
2   teaspoons ground pumpkin pie spice
½   cup butter, softened
1½ cups firmly packed brown sugar
2   eggs
1   cup cooked or canned pumpkin
1   teaspoon vanilla
1½ cups coarsely chopped walnuts

Preheat oven to 375° F. In a medium bowl, sift together flour, baking powder, and pumpkin pie spice; set aside. In a large bowl, cream butter with brown sugar until light and fluffy. Beat in eggs, one at a time; stir in pumpkin and vanilla. Add flour mixture; mix well. Stir in walnuts. Drop by rounded teaspoons 1 inch apart onto greased baking sheets. Bake in upper third of oven 12 to 14 minutes. Cool on wire racks.

Pear Brown Betty
Makes 6 servings

4   cups peeled, sliced pears
1   cup raisins
¼   cup orange juice
1   cup sugar
¾   cup flour
½   teaspoon ground cinnamon
¼   teaspoon ground nutmeg
½   cup butter
    Ice cream or whipping cream

Preheat oven to 375° F. In an 8-inch-square baking pan, combine pears, raisins, and orange juice; set aside. In a large bowl, combine sugar, flour, cinnamon, and nutmeg; mix well. Using a pastry blender or fork, cut in butter until mixture resembles coarse crumbs. Sprinkle evenly over pear mixture. Bake 45 minutes or until lightly browned. Serve warm or at room temperature with ice cream or whipping cream.

Southern Custard Pecan Pie
Makes 10 servings

1   cup sugar
1   cup firmly packed, light brown sugar
¾   cup egg substitute
2   tablespoons melted butter
1   teaspoon vanilla
1   cup pecan halves
1   9-inch unbaked pie shell

Preheat oven to 400° F. In a large bowl, combine sugar, brown sugar, egg substitute, butter, and vanilla; mix well. Stir in pecans. Pour mixture into pie shell. Bake at 400° F for 15 minutes. Reduce oven temperature to 350° F and bake 25 to 30 minutes more or until lightly browned and completely puffed across top of pie. Cool completely on wire rack.

Banana Pumpkin Pie
Makes 10 servings

2   ripe bananas, mashed (about ¾ cup)
1   cup canned pumpkin
1   12-ounce can evaporated skim milk
1   egg
1   cup sugar
1   teaspoon ground pumpkin pie spice
1   9-inch graham cracker pie shell

Preheat oven to 400° F. In a large bowl, combine bananas, pumpkin, milk, egg, sugar, and spice; mix well. Place pie shell on a baking sheet and pour mixture into shell. Bake at 400° F for 15 minutes. Reduce oven temperature to 350° F and bake 40 to 45 minutes more or until knife inserted in center comes out clean. Cool completely on wire rack. Serve at room temperature or chilled.

FLOURISHES: *Sugared fruits are an exquisite garnish for desserts. Choose small fruits such as grapes and kumquats. Using a small brush, apply a thin coat of lightly beaten egg white to the fruits. Sprinkle with granulated sugar and dry for several hours on a wire rack.*

Christmas

Chocolate Christmas Confections

Makes 2½ dozen

- 2 cups vanilla wafer crumbs
- ½ cup powdered sugar
- ½ cup chopped walnuts
- 2 teaspoons instant coffee granules
- ¼ cup boiling water
- 2 tablespoons butter
- 1 tablespoon light corn syrup
- 30 maraschino cherries with stems, well drained
- 2 6-ounce packages semisweet chocolate chips
  - Flaked coconut
  - Multicolored sprinkles
  - Chocolate sprinkles
  - Finely chopped nuts

In a large bowl, combine vanilla wafer crumbs, sugar, and walnuts; set aside. In a small bowl, dissolve coffee in water; add butter and corn syrup. Add coffee mixture to crumb mixture; mix thoroughly. Shape approximately 1 rounded teaspoon of mixture around each cherry, coating fingers with powdered sugar to prevent sticking. Cover and refrigerate at least 1 hour.

Place a wire rack over a layer of wax paper. In a double boiler, melt chocolate chips over hot water. Holding stem, carefully dip each cherry into chocolate, coating completely. Place coated cherries on wire rack. Cool 5 minutes; garnish with coconut, sprinkles, or nuts. Refrigerate until chocolate hardens.

Gingerbread Cookies

Makes 4 dozen

- 4½ cups flour
- 2 teaspoons baking soda
- 2 teaspoons ground cinnamon
- 2 teaspoons ground ginger
- ½ teaspoon ground cloves
- ½ teaspoon ground nutmeg
- ½ cup butter, softened
- ¾ cup firmly packed, light brown sugar
- ¼ cup egg substitute
- ¾ cup light molasses
- 1 cup powdered sugar
- 5½ teaspoons skim milk
  - Assorted small candies

In a medium bowl, sift together flour, baking soda, and spices; set aside. In a large bowl, cream butter with brown sugar until light and fluffy. Beat in egg substitute and molasses. Stir in flour mixture to make a stiff dough. Divide dough in half; wrap and chill for several hours or overnight.

Preheat oven to 350° F. Roll out a small amount of dough onto well greased and floured baking sheets. Cut with 4-inch cookie cutters. Remove scraps and roll again. Bake 8 to 10 minutes or just until set and lightly brown. Cool completely on wire racks. In a small bowl, combine powdered sugar and skim milk. Spread mixture on cookies and decorate with assorted small candies.

Peanut Butter Brownies (page 29), All-in-One Cookies (page 28), and Nut Brittle Cookie Bars (page 28)

Nut Brittle Cookie Bars
Makes 4 dozen

1⅔ cups flour
¾ teaspoon baking powder
½ cup cold butter
2 tablespoons sugar
1 egg, slightly beaten
2 tablespoons evaporated milk
1 10-ounce package peanut butter chips, divided
    Nut Filling (recipe follows)

Preheat oven to 375° F. In a medium bowl, sift together flour and baking powder; set aside. In a large bowl, cream butter with sugar until light and fluffy. Add flour mixture; mix well. Stir in egg and evaporated milk; stir until mixture holds together. Press evenly onto bottom and up sides of a 15½-by-10½-by-1-inch jelly roll pan. Bake 8 to 10 minutes or until golden; cool in pan on wire rack. Sprinkle 1 cup of the peanut butter chips over crust. Prepare Nut Filling; carefully spoon over baked crust and chips (do not spread; mixture will spread during baking). Bake 12 to 15 minutes or until filling is caramel colored. Sprinkle remaining ⅔ cup peanut butter chips over top. Cool completely in pan on wire rack; cut into bars.

Nut Filling

1½ cups sugar
½ cup butter
½ cup evaporated milk
½ cup light corn syrup
1½ cups sliced almonds

In a 3-quart saucepan, place sugar, butter, evaporated milk, and corn syrup. Place over medium heat, stirring constantly, until mixture boils; stir in almonds. Continue cooking and stirring over medium heat until mixture reaches 240° F on a candy thermometer or to the soft ball stage when mixture forms a soft ball when dropped into cold water. Remove from heat; use immediately.

All-in-One Cookies
Makes about 5 dozen

2½ cups flour
1 teaspoon baking soda
½ teaspoon salt
1 cup butter, softened
1 cup sugar
¾ cup packed, light brown sugar
2 teaspoons vanilla
2 eggs
1 10-ounce package chocolate chips

Preheat oven to 375° F. In a small bowl, sift together flour, baking soda, and salt; set aside. In a large bowl, with electric mixer, cream butter with sugar and brown sugar until light and fluffy. Add vanilla and eggs; beat well. Gradually add flour mixture, beating until well mixed. Stir in chocolate chips. Drop by rounded teaspoons onto ungreased baking sheets. Bake 8 to 10 minutes or until set. Cool slightly; remove to wire racks.

Holiday Marmalade
Fills about five 12-ounce jars

1 fresh pineapple, cored, peeled, and finely chopped
2 oranges, seeded and ground
2 lemons, seeded and ground
5 cups sugar
1 12-ounce package frozen tart red cherries
½ cup shredded coconut

Prepare home canning jars and lids according to manufacturer's instructions. In a large saucepan, combine pineapple, oranges, lemons, and sugar. Bring mixture to a boil, stirring until sugar is dissolved. Cook rapidly to 220° F, about 40 minutes. Add cherries and coconut; cook 10 more minutes. Carefully ladle hot marmalade into sterile jars, leaving ¼-inch headspace. Wipe jar rim clean. Replace jar lids and bands evenly and firmly. Do not use excessive force. Process 10 minutes in a boiling-water canner.

Peanut Butter Brownies
Makes about 3 dozen

1¾ cups flour
1 teaspoon baking powder
⅔ cup butter, softened
¾ cup peanut butter
½ cup sugar
1 cup packed, light brown sugar
2 eggs
1 teaspoon vanilla
⅓ cup milk
2¼ cups chocolate candy KISSES, divided
½ teaspoon vegetable shortening

Preheat oven to 325° F. In a small bowl, sift together flour and baking powder; set aside. In a large bowl, cream butter and peanut butter with sugar and brown sugar until light and fluffy. Add eggs and vanilla; beat well. Gradually beat in milk. Slowly beat in flour mixture; mix well. Spread half of batter into a greased 13-by-9-by-2-inch baking pan; spread 2 cups of the chocolate KISSES over batter. Spread remaining batter over chocolate, covering completely. Bake 40 to 45 minutes or until wooden pick inserted in center comes out clean. Cool completely in pan on wire rack.

In a small microwave-safe bowl, place remaining ½ cup chocolate KISSES and shortening (not butter, margarine, or oil). Microwave at high power (100%) 30 seconds or just until melted when stirred. Drizzle over brownies. Cut into bars.

Holiday Sugar Cookies
Makes 3½ dozen

2 cups flour
1½ teaspoons baking soda
½ cup butter, softened
1 cup sugar, divided
2 teaspoons grated orange peel
1 teaspoon vanilla
¼ cup egg substitute
   Assorted small candies
   Colored sprinkles

In a small bowl, sift together flour and baking soda; set aside. In a large bowl, with electric mixer on medium speed, cream butter with ¾ cup of the sugar until light and fluffy. Add orange peel and vanilla. Add egg substitute; beat for 1 minute. Gradually stir in flour mixture until blended. Chill dough for 1 hour.

Preheat oven to 375° F. Shape dough into forty-two ¾-inch balls; roll balls in remaining ¼ cup sugar. Place 2 inches apart on lightly greased baking sheets. Flatten with the bottom of a glass. Bake 8 to 10 minutes or until lightly browned. Cool on wire racks. Decorate with assorted candies and colored sprinkles. Wrap and store at room temperature for up to 1 week.

Browned Butter Crunch Cake
Makes 12 servings

1 cup finely chopped walnuts, divided
½ cup plus 1 tablespoon sugar, divided
1 cup butter
1 cup firmly packed brown sugar
2 eggs
2 teaspoons vanilla
2¼ cups flour
1 teaspoon baking powder
½ teaspoon baking soda
¾ cup milk

Preheat oven to 350° F. Grease a 10-inch tube pan. Coat pan evenly with ⅔ cup of the walnuts; sprinkle walnuts with 1 tablespoon of the sugar; set aside. In a small saucepan, melt butter over medium heat, stirring occasionally, until bubbling and golden brown. In a large bowl, combine browned butter, remaining ½ cup sugar, brown sugar, eggs, and vanilla; blend well and set aside. In a large bowl, sift together flour, baking powder, and baking soda; add to butter mixture alternately with milk. Pour into prepared pan; sprinkle with remaining ⅓ cup walnuts. Bake 40 minutes or until wooden pick inserted in center comes out clean. Cool in pan 10 minutes. Remove from pan and cool on wire rack.

Cherry Cheese Bars
Makes 3 dozen

¾ cup butter, softened
¾ cup sugar
2 eggs, divided
1½ cups plus 2 to 4 tablespoons flour, divided
¼ teaspoon salt
1 8-ounce package cream cheese, softened
1 cup cherry preserves

Preheat oven to 350° F. In a large bowl, with electric mixer, cream butter with sugar until light and fluffy. Add one egg; beat well. Stir in 1½ cups flour and the salt until well blended. In a medium bowl, reserve 1 cup of mixture; set aside. Press remaining crust mixture into a greased 13-by-9-by-2-inch baking pan (dust fingers with flour for easier handling). Bake 15 minutes. Blend remaining 2 to 4 tablespoons flour into reserved crust mixture until crumbly; set aside.

In a small bowl, with electric mixer, blend cream cheese and remaining egg until smooth. Spread cream cheese mixture evenly over baked crust. Spoon cherry preserves over cream cheese mixture. Sprinkle with reserved crumb topping. Bake 35 to 40 minutes or until edges are golden brown. Cool on wire rack before cutting.

Black Forest Banana Cupcakes
Makes 2 dozen

1 8-ounce package light cream cheese, softened
1 egg
1¾ cups sugar, divided
⅓ cup candied cherries, chopped
¼ cup miniature semisweet chocolate chips
2 cups flour
⅓ cup cocoa
1½ teaspoons baking powder
2 ripe bananas, mashed (about ¾ cup)
⅓ cup vegetable oil
¾ cup water

Preheat oven to 350° F. In a small bowl, beat cream cheese until smooth. Add egg and ¼ cup of the sugar; beat until blended. Stir in cherries and chocolate chips; set aside.

In a medium bowl, sift together flour, cocoa, and baking powder; set aside. In a large bowl, combine bananas, oil, and water. Add remaining 1½ cups sugar. Add flour mixture; stir until well blended. Spoon banana mixture evenly into 24 muffin cups lined with paper cups. Spoon about 1 tablespoon cream cheese mixture onto center of each cupcake. Bake 25 to 30 minutes or until wooden pick inserted in center comes out clean. Remove from pan; cool completely on wire rack.

Walnut Fudge Bread Pudding
Makes 4 to 6 servings

1½ cups milk
1 6-ounce package semisweet chocolate chips
¾ cup sugar
1 tablespoon butter
1 egg, slightly beaten
1½ cups coarse, fresh bread crumbs
1 cup chopped walnuts

Preheat oven to 350° F. In a medium saucepan, combine milk, chocolate chips, and sugar. Place over low heat until chocolate is melted and mixture is smooth. Remove from heat and stir in butter. Slowly stir in egg. Stir in bread crumbs and walnuts. Pour into a greased 1-quart baking pan. Place pan into a 13-by-9-inch, metal baking pan. Set pans on oven rack. Pour 1 inch hot water into larger pan, surrounding 1-quart pan. Bake 45 to 50 minutes or until knife inserted 1 inch from edge comes out clean.

FLOURISHES: *Strawberry stars brighten any holiday dessert. Start with several ripe, hulled strawberries of similar size. Slice each berry in half lengthwise; then slice each half lengthwise again. Connect the rounded ends of five berry slices to form a star shape. Tuck a mint leaf to the side for added color.*

Index

Our sincere thanks to the following companies for their cooperation in supplying recipes and photographs: Consumer Products Company, Alltrista Corporation; Dole Food Company; Hershey Foods Corporation; Kellogg Company; Ketchum Public Relations and the California Strawberry Commission; Martha White; Nabisco; The Quaker Oats Company; and Sun-Diamond Growers of California.

PHOTOGRAPHY CREDITS

Cover, Jessie Walker Associates; **Page 3,** Dole Food Company; **7,** Hershey Foods Corporation; **11,** The Quaker Oats Company; **15,** Alan Ross/California Strawberry Commission; **19,** The Quaker Oats Company; **23,** Hershey Foods Corporation; **27,** Hershey Foods Corporation; **31,** Dole Food Company.

A 1
B 2
C 3
D 4
E 5
F 6
G 7
H 8
I 9
J 0